Beyond the Expectations

Learning to Obey

Dave Wager

Foreword by Jack D. Eggar,
President/CEO of Awana

Grace Acres Press
P.O. Box 22
Larkspur, CO 80118
888-700-GRACE (4722)
(303) 681-9995
(303) 681-9996 fax
www.GraceAcresPress.com

CULTIVATING JOY

Grace Acres Press also publishes books in a variety of
electronic formats. Some content that appears in print may
not be available in electronic books.

Throughout this book, we use the following abbreviations:

NIV   *New International Version*

Scripture taken from the *Holy Bible, New International Version.*®
NIV.® Copyright © 1973, 1978, 1984 by International Bible
Society. Used by permission of Zondervan Publishing House.
All rights reserved.

NLT   *New Living Testament*

Holy Bible, New Living Translation. Copyright © 1996
by Tyndale Charitable Trust. All rights reserved. Database
copyright © 1997 NavPress Software.

Library of Congress Cataloging-in-Publication Data:
Wager, Dave, 1956–
   Beyond the expectations : learning to obey / by Dave
Wager.
       p.   cm.
   ISBN: 978-1-60265-014-5
       1. Expectation (Psychology)—Religious aspects—
Christianity. 2. Trust in God. 3. Teenagers—Religious life.
I. Title.
   BV4647.E93W34   2008
   242—dc22
                                                      2008032940

Printed in the United States of America
12 11 10 09   01 02 03 04 05 06 07 08 09 10

Praise for *Beyond the Expectations*

*A distorted view of God or life's challenges can derail
any of us from our Christian life and service. Dave
Wager's book provides biblical and practical insights that
bring encouragement and a proper focus.*

> NELSON MILES
> President, Frontier School of the Bible

Beyond the Expectations: Learning to Obey *is biblical,
direct, insightful, challenging, and a clarion call to obey
Christ beyond the masks we are tempted to wear—a lot
like its author, Dave Wager. The pithy questions, the
thought-provoking illustrations, and the faithful foundation
of Scriptural truth make this volume a wise and powerful
goad to authentic Christian discipleship.*

> GREGORY C. CARLSON, PHD
> Chair and Professor of Christian
> Ministries, Trinity International
> University

*Let's face it. Life can be cruel. Sometimes you get a
curveball when you were expecting a fastball. And when
those unexpected curveballs come, you can either duck and
swerve, or stay focused and give it a try. In the end, the
difference between a strike and a home run often comes
down to what Dave Wager calls the misery index: that gap
between your expectations and reality. In his encouraging
new book,* Beyond the Expectations, *Wager uses the
examples of several biblical men and women to illustrate
the importance of trusting God, not your own expectations.
He reminds us that sometimes life's greatest blessings come
wrapped in hardship. Loaded with rich biblical anecdotes
and solid life principles, Wager's book is a must for anyone*

who knows what it's like to swing and miss. Beyond the
Expectations *will help you step back up to the plate and
swing with confidence . . . in the Lord!*

> J. B. HIXSON, PhD
> Executive Director, Free Grace Alliance

*I believe many people serve Jesus because of the hope they
receive from Him. However, they hope in Jesus for things,
instead of just putting their trust in God. They treat Him
like a year-round Santa Claus, rather than as the Creator
of the universe. Then, when they don't get what they hope
for, their "faith" in Jesus disappears. Or was it never
there to begin with? Dave Wager nails it in his new book,*
Beyond the Expectations. *Read it and fall in love with
God for who He really is. This book will help produce
lasting, faithful disciples of our Lord Jesus. Get it.*

> BOB LENZ
> Speaker and author of *Grace—For
> Those Who Think They Don't Measure Up*

*If you are just getting started—beginning a relationship,
entering a ministry, starting a new job, or just embarking
on your walk of faith—this book is for you! Or, if you
have been around the block—having been hurt and
disappointed, or becoming resentful and disillusioned—
this book is for you! In either case, these thoughts
concerning your expectations of others and theirs of you
will stimulate, challenge, and comfort you.*

> JEFF ANDERSON
> Grace Bible Church, Colorado Springs

This book is dedicated to my wife, Linda, who has been my partner, friend, and love for many years. Since our early days, she has been a pillar of sound advice as she has helped me sort out truth from error. In a world where there is much disappointment in unfulfilled expectations, Linda has lived in a way that has gone beyond my expectations. I am indeed a better leader today because she is my partner.

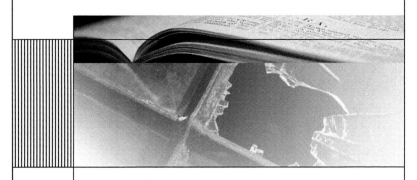

2 Corinthians 1:8–10 (NLT)

8 WE THINK YOU OUGHT TO KNOW, DEAR BROTHERS AND SISTERS, ABOUT THE TROUBLE WE WENT THROUGH IN THE PROVINCE OF ASIA. WE WERE CRUSHED AND OVERWHELMED BEYOND OUR ABILITY TO ENDURE, AND WE THOUGHT WE WOULD NEVER LIVE THROUGH IT.

9 IN FACT, WE EXPECTED TO DIE. BUT AS A RESULT, WE STOPPED RELYING ON OURSELVES AND LEARNED TO RELY ONLY ON GOD, WHO RAISES THE DEAD.

10 AND HE DID RESCUE US FROM MORTAL DANGER, AND HE WILL RESCUE US AGAIN. WE HAVE PLACED OUR CONFIDENCE IN HIM, AND HE WILL CONTINUE TO RESCUE US.

Contents

About the Author

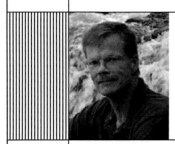

For the past twenty-five years, Dave Wager has served as a leader, friend, and teacher to thousands who have entered the educational grounds of Silver Birch Ranch in White Lake, Wisconsin. Today Dave continues to serve as the president of Silver Birch Ranch, and also teaches at camps, conferences, churches, and businesses throughout the world.

Dave's life has been dedicated to the growth of young people, first as a volunteer youth worker and then later as a fifth-grade teacher. He has served as president of the Wisconsin Christian Camping Association and currently teaches a class in "Christian Life and Ethics" at the Nicolet Bible Institute. Dave holds a B.A. from Wheaton College and an M.S. Ed. from Northern Illinois University.

Dave desires that each person he meets walk intimately with God and fulfill the purposes for which he or she was designed. He believes that joy and effectiveness in life, work, and ministry come from knowing what really matters. His focus is in examining how today's choices affect the real bottom line: knowing what we are about, what are our responsibilities, and what are God's responsibilities.

Foreword

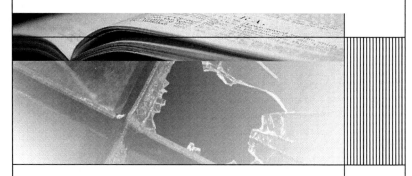

We all have expectations of ourselves, of others, and even of God—especially of God, if we are to be honest. Surely, if we are walking closely with Him and obeying His commands, He should bless us with health, wealth, happiness—and let's not forget about the safety of our loved ones, risk-free living, and every imaginable success. Our stocks should not fall, our health should not fail, and our service should be rewarded immediately, if not sooner! Thank You very much, Lord!

In *Beyond the Expectations,* my good friend Dave Wager reveals a different reality about God that we sometimes overlook. A blessing from the Lord may not look like a blessing to a man. This has been proven numerous times in the lives of the people we have come to know so intimately in Scripture, from Joseph and Ezekiel to Mary and Abraham.

Dave's book will inspire you to rethink your expectations of the Lord, your understanding of blessings, and your level of obedience. In other words, it will do a number on your mind. But isn't that exactly what Paul intended in ROMANS 12:1–2 when he said to be transformed by the renewing of our minds? Only then will we be able to prove what is God's good, acceptable, and perfect will for us. So what awaits those who do test and prove such things? Rest! I'm not talking about taking a nap. This

rest comes only through a deep, abiding faith. Have you ever experienced such a thing?

The more time we spend with our Creator and Master, the more our expectations align with His. Disappointments and demands are replaced by unspeakable joy and peace.

I highly recommend Dave's book to anyone who desires a more personal, realistic, biblically grounded relationship with God. May we all learn to take full pleasure in the honor of being called His friends.

JACK D. EGGAR
Awana President/CEO

Acknowledgments

There are always a few who seem able to live their lives beyond any human expectation. It is those leaders who have lived, written, preached, exhorted, pleaded, and demonstrated lives who both challenged and encouraged me to live my life beyond the expectations.

First on that list of leaders would be both my mom, Joyce, and my dad, Rich. Closely following are my brother, Rick, and my wife, Linda. Then there are those who have ministered together at Silver Birch Ranch for more than 15 years: Roberta Berggren, Dan Betz, Brad Ellis, Rich Hess, Tom Huska, Dave Lupella, Loren Mytas, and Steve Sanford; as well as those who started the year-round work at Silver Birch Ranch: Dave Bradley, Ron and Ruth Elwardt, and Ken Henley.

God uses people to demonstrate his timeless truths, and to each of those listed I owe a measure of thanks for their faithfulness to God in their everyday lives. They have lived, and I believe will continue to live, beyond the expectations!

Introduction

There once was a young lady who often dreamed of the day she would be married. The plan was to marry a well-to-do young man who was polite, kind, and generous, and who would adore her. He would be her knight in shining armor, and he would protect her, love her, nurture her, and provide for her. They would live in a rather nice house in the outskirts of a major city (one with a big yard for a big dog!), and be a part of the social elite. They would go to a big church, with a big choir, and be active members looking for opportunities to give and to serve.

Finally, her wedding day comes, and she is excited about beginning her dream life. It is not long, though, before her expectations are dashed; months after they are married, they are living in a small two-room apartment, in the inner city, that does not allow pets. Her husband, she finds out, has been living a secret life, neglects God and her, and does not even want to attend a church full of hypocrites. She feels more used than loved, and the church they attend spends more time talking about them than to them.

The gap between what is expected in life and what is realized is what is called the "misery index," and this young lady has developed quite an index. Because we frequently base our lives on what we understand, hope for, and dream about, we are often disappointed in what

really happens or what is actually delivered. We expect certain results from our actions, so we work the plan we have while we make a better plan. This would be well and good in a situation in which we were actually the ones who controlled all the variables—but we do *not* control all the variables. In fact, there is much more that we do not control than we do control. There is a great deal that we need to understand that we do not and cannot understand.

Many people today live miserable lives because they have a huge misery index to deal with. They have a false understanding of God, a false understanding of love, a false understanding of blessing, a false understanding of friendship . . . and they are totally lost when it comes to purpose. In fact, those who are most miserable are those who spend their lives in the context of their own understanding. Our understanding of life, circumstances, and purpose is quite limited. We need to be intimate enough with God to actually know that His love for us has been demonstrated, and will be demonstrated in a way that is consistent with His character.

Satan will take the opposite approach, trying to put us into a tail-spin of self-pity that is fueled by our false and unfounded expectations. He accomplishes most of his evil work by encouraging us to view life through the lens of our own understanding, feelings, plans, and purposes.

I hope this book will help you spend time thinking about what lies beyond our human expectations, and aids you in doing away with any misery indexes you have created.

Thought for Day 1

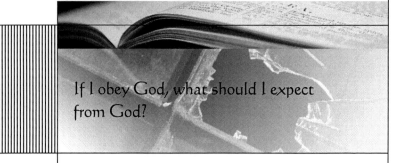

If I obey God, what should I expect from God?

John 13:18–19 (NLT)

18 "I AM NOT SAYING THESE THINGS TO ALL OF YOU; I KNOW THE ONES I HAVE CHOSEN. BUT THIS FULFILLS THE SCRIPTURE THAT SAYS, 'THE ONE WHO EATS MY FOOD HAS TURNED AGAINST ME.'

19 I TELL YOU THIS BEFOREHAND, SO THAT WHEN IT HAPPENS YOU WILL BELIEVE THAT I AM THE MESSIAH.

How could anyone turn against Jesus? How could someone who had walked with Him, seen His miracles, or heard His messages ever turn against Him?

Could it be that Judas' expectation of what he was to receive by following Jesus was finally brought into the light of day and reality? It seems as if Judas had a different idea, a different expectation, a different hope and dream about what a disciple should receive. Judas was, by all accounts, one of the most educated and trusted disciples. He was the one who was in charge of the "bag," or the money. He was the one who was concerned with paying the bills. He was the one, should Jesus become a physical king and ruler, who would hold the most powerful position of authority in the kingdom. He was well positioned to take personal advantage of Jesus' ascent to power.

Now, all of a sudden, the picture was changing. Jesus was making it clear that he had not come to rule, but to die. Jesus was washing the disciples' feet and was talking some "nonsense" about coming to serve and not be served. This is not what Judas had bargained for. This was not the stuff his dreams were made of, and his personal misery index began to grow.

Apparently, Judas actually thought that following Christ would one day make him rich, powerful, and respected, when in reality, it would make him poor, powerless, and hunted. Judas did what anyone would do who is profoundly disappointed in the circumstances of life: he tried to close the misery gap by going to those who would listen to him, exalt him, and—most importantly —pay him.

He sold out to Christ's enemies. I guess he thought he would show Christ that He should not have disappointed him. He would show the world what kind of power he yielded. Judas got what he thought he was looking for, for a moment. He got to hobnob with the people who were in power; he got to help them arrest Jesus. He got, at least for the moment, praise and adulation. Most of all, though, he got money.

The thing he did not get was satisfaction. In fact, the things he thought would bring satisfaction drove true satisfaction further away than he ever thought possible. His misery index grew to the point of total despair.

Like all those who hope to find ultimate satisfaction in the things of this temporal life, Judas became hopelessly depressed.

 What is it you expect from God?
What should you expect?

THOUGHT FOR DAY 1

5

Thought for Day 2

There is a time when you know that
Jesus is God.

Luke 22:61–62 (NLT)

61 AT THAT MOMENT THE LORD TURNED AND LOOKED
AT PETER. THEN PETER REMEMBERED THAT THE LORD
HAD SAID, "BEFORE THE ROOSTER CROWS TOMORROW
MORNING, YOU WILL DENY THREE TIMES THAT YOU EVEN
KNOW ME."

62 AND PETER LEFT THE COURTYARD, WEEPING BITTERLY.

Peter too seemed disillusioned, to a point. He never
believed that he would deny Christ. He proudly
proclaimed that he would stand by Jesus' side no matter
what the circumstances. Jesus knew otherwise.

I imagine Peter knew that Jesus was indeed God, and
perhaps that was the problem. How could Jesus, God,
allow this to happen? How could the God of the universe
allow people whom He had created to put Him to trial,
to beat Him, and eventually to crucify Him? How could
all of this pain be a part of victory? How does all of this
fit with what Jesus said and did?

Peter's thoughts must have been racing as he stood
warming himself by that charcoal fire. As people came

and recognized him as a follower of Jesus, he kept saying that he did not know the man, and I think he might actually have been telling the truth. I think at this point Peter's hopes, dreams, and very idea of God were being dashed. He honestly thought that this man Jesus was God—yet how could God allow such things to happen? There was a moment of temporary disillusionment, until the rooster crowed, and Jesus' eyes met Peter's eyes.

Once again, in the moment of his greatest personal despair, Peter was reminded that Jesus was indeed God. All it took was a rooster and a glance.

Unlike Judas, though, when Peter's misery index started to grow, Peter went to where he could find the answers. He did not run, and he did not hide, even though he did deny. Because he hung around where the answers were, when the time came for the answer to be revealed, he was there, and he was responsive. That was a critical moment in Peter's life, a moment when he understood that Jesus was indeed who He said He was. It was a moment that began to close the misery gap in an honest and healthful manner.

Jesus did not come to this earth and die to make things easy for us. He came to lead and equip us for battle. During our time on earth, we battle. When we die, if we were on the right side, we rest victoriously.

Those who think that following Christ will bring them health, fame, fortune, and comfort are in for a profound disappointment. Satan offers these things as a substitute for real peace and purpose, but, in reality, they never satisfy.

All of us have some unfulfilled expectations concerning how God should treat us.

This disappointment can either lead us to despair and rash actions, or propel us to leadership. What is it doing in your life?

_____

_____

_____

_____

_____

_____

_____

_____

_____

_____

_____

_____

_____

_____

_____

_____

_____

Thought for Day 3

Our past will paralyze us or propel us
in our leadership role.

John 21:15–17 (NLT)

15 AFTER BREAKFAST JESUS ASKED SIMON PETER,
"SIMON SON OF JOHN, DO YOU LOVE ME MORE THAN
THESE?" "YES, LORD," PETER REPLIED, "YOU KNOW I
LOVE YOU." "THEN FEED MY LAMBS," JESUS TOLD HIM.

16 JESUS REPEATED THE QUESTION: "SIMON SON OF JOHN,
DO YOU LOVE ME?" "YES, LORD," PETER SAID, "YOU KNOW
I LOVE YOU." "THEN TAKE CARE OF MY SHEEP," JESUS SAID.

17 THIRD TIME HE ASKED HIM, "SIMON SON OF JOHN,
DO YOU LOVE ME?" PETER WAS HURT THAT JESUS ASKED
THE QUESTION A THIRD TIME. HE SAID, "LORD, YOU
KNOW EVERYTHING. YOU KNOW THAT I LOVE YOU." JESUS
SAID, "THEN FEED MY SHEEP."

Peter seemed to really know that Jesus was God when
the rooster crowed and his eyes met those of Jesus, but
these occurrences must have left him wondering. He
must have wondered whether he had lost his qualifica-
tions for leadership among the disciples. He must
have wondered if God could ever use a man who would
deny Him in public. He must have wondered why he,
such a strong man, had given into such relatively minor
pressure. He must have wondered about his friendship
with Jesus, and where they now stood.

So, like any self-respecting man, he went back to what he knew how to do: fishing. Once again, Jesus met Peter where he was, and helped him finish closing the misery gap he had created for himself. As Peter and others fished, Jesus appeared on the shore. He asked them, as friendly folks often do, how the fishing was going, and they responded negatively, that it was not going well. Jesus told them to cast their nets on the other side, and they did. John told Peter that it was Jesus, and Peter swam to Jesus, who had a charcoal fire going on the shore.

Now, I may be reading too much into this story, but there seem to be only two times in the New Testament that a charcoal fire is mentioned. The first time is when Peter stood around one and denied Christ. The second time is when Christ wanted to talk with Peter and reaffirm that Peter was specially called to lead the new church. This was probably no accident: a charcoal fire gives heat, of course, but it also has a distinctive scent. Human senses, especially the sense of smell, are powerful memory stimulants, and Jesus seemed to be reminding Peter of another moment in history that perhaps Peter was trying to move past.

As they stood there, Jesus asked Peter three times if Peter loved Him. It seems like Jesus was rubbing it in— or was He fostering the healing process?

Jesus knew where Peter's heart was, and He knew that Peter felt like a failure. Nevertheless, Jesus did not let Peter weasel out of his responsibility just because he had more growing-up to do. Each time, after Peter was questioned, Jesus told him to feed His sheep. He did not say, "Peter, when you finally arrive at perfection, feed my sheep." He did not say, "Peter, when you finally grow to a certain point, feed my sheep." Jesus' insistence instead seemed to imply, "Peter, I know where you are at. I know your shortcomings. I know your capabilities. Go and feed my sheep."

Sometimes I want to wait until I know enough, until I am holy enough, or until I am disciplined enough to serve God. Sometimes, because of my failures, I expect God to strike me down and not use me. What are your expectations about who God uses? Would He actually use you? Why?

_____

_____

_____

_____

_____

_____

_____

_____

_____

_____

_____

_____

_____

Thought for Day 4

Should those who follow Jesus actually be radical in their thinking, radical in their giving, and radical in their service to others?

Matthew 19:21–22 (NLT)

21 JESUS TOLD HIM, "IF YOU WANT TO BE PERFECT, GO AND SELL ALL YOUR POSSESSIONS AND GIVE THE MONEY TO THE POOR, AND YOU WILL HAVE TREASURE IN HEAVEN. THEN COME, FOLLOW ME."

22 BUT WHEN THE YOUNG MAN HEARD THIS, HE WENT AWAY VERY SAD, FOR HE HAD MANY POSSESSIONS.

Sometimes God is portrayed as a sort of genie in a bottle. We come to Him with our agendas, and He acts on our behalf, granting our wishes, as long as we somewhat behave. If God is a part of our lives, we expect to be blessed, to have stuff, to laugh a lot, party a lot, and, well, be self-indulgent a lot.

This is a lie from the pit of hell. All throughout the Bible we are told to live lives dependent upon God. We have money, but we are not to depend upon it. We have friends, but we are not to depend upon them. We have health, but we are not to depend upon it. We have homes, but we are not to depend upon them. We have education, but we are not to depend upon it.

The rich young man in the verse may have been one who was more honest than most. He probably realized that his human popularity was based on his wealth, as

were his comfort, purpose, and plans. If he were to give away his wealth, he would be giving away his status, comfort, and perceived purpose.

What is it in my life that brings me status, comfort, and purpose? What in my life is so important to me that I would not give it up, even if God Himself gave me the order to do so?

Of course, I would like to answer "nothing" to this question, but I would probably be lying to myself. I need to take some time and examine what I find important, the "nonnegotiables" of my human existence, and see if they are in line with what I find in the Bible.

Anything that I trust in, other than God, is my god. Anything I live for, other than God, is something I have spiritually prostituted myself to.

I really do not spend much time identifying myself with this rich young man, because I am not a rich young man. I realize that I am made right with God by faith, not by works, so I am not too concerned with God's judgment of my sin. (I know full well that Jesus died to redeem me and that my sins are forgiven.) Still, I see the principle very clearly.

Before I come to Christ, there are things in my life that will prevent me from coming to Him. After I come to Christ, there will be things that prevent me from totally following and trusting Him. Am I even capable of identifying these things and rectifying the situation?

God, help me as I try to be honest about what might be hindering me, and forgive me for so often having the wrong expectation of what I deserve for my limited trust and obedience.

What is hindering your total obedience?
What are you going to do about it?

_____

_____

_____

_____

_____

_____

_____

_____

_____

_____

_____

_____

_____

_____

_____

_____

_____

Thought for Day 5

How does God keep me from trusting in things?

1 Kings 17:2–4 (NLT)

2 Then the Lord said to Elijah,

3 "Go to the east and hide by Kerith Brook, near where it enters the Jordan River.

4 Drink from the brook and eat what the ravens bring you, for I have commanded them to bring you food."

What can I expect when I follow God?

Elijah followed God, and God provided. That seems to make total sense. When all around were dying because of drought, Elijah was eating with ravens. . . . How cool is that?

But there came a time when the brook dried and the ravens quit bringing food. What is the deal with *that*? Why would God provide and then stop providing? What is God up to when He does such things?

I am not sure, because the Bible is not clear about this. It just tells us that the brook dried up and the ravens quit bringing food. God's provisionary plan was then shifted to a widow who was down to her last meal. Elijah met

her and asked her to cook her last provisions for him. She did, and God miraculously intervened once again by making sure that her supply of flour and oil did not run out.

I can imagine that both Elijah and this widow and her son celebrated in the streets over the provisions God had supplied. But then an apparently awful thing happened: After these miraculous provisions, the widow's son died unexpectedly.

Can you imagine the feelings of Elijah and the widow? Here God was demonstrating His faithfulness in an obvious and wonderful way, and suddenly the most important reason for the provision—at least for the widow—was taken from her by something other than starvation.

What would you be thinking?

I think my personal misery index would be shooting up. It would be growing because I would have expected the flour and oil to keep my family alive. Once again, I would have actually placed my trust in the provision rather than the provider.

I am not sure, but it would be reasonable to surmise that Elijah got used to the provision of the brook and the ravens, and expected the brook and the ravens to care for him. It would have been easy to forget God, and to trust instead in what God gave. The widow, too, was probably thinking that she had it made now that her food needs were met. She probably began to trust in the flour and oil to keep her and her family alive. She found out that life is sustained not by grain, but by God.

I wonder if there are things in my life, gifts from God, that I have started to trust in.

I wonder if the expectation I have in the provision is now greater than my faith in the provider. Are there things God has given you that you now trust?

_____

_____

_____

_____

_____

_____

_____

_____

_____

_____

_____

_____

_____

_____

_____

_____

Thought for Day 6

What does one who seeks God wholeheartedly look like?

2 Chronicles 31:20–21 (NLT)

20 IN THIS WAY, KING HEZEKIAH HANDLED THE DISTRIBUTION THROUGHOUT ALL JUDAH, DOING WHAT WAS PLEASING AND GOOD IN THE SIGHT OF THE LORD HIS GOD.

21 IN ALL THAT HE DID IN THE SERVICE OF THE TEMPLE OF GOD AND IN HIS EFFORTS TO FOLLOW GOD'S LAWS AND COMMANDS, HEZEKIAH SOUGHT HIS GOD WHOLEHEARTEDLY. AS A RESULT, HE WAS VERY SUCCESSFUL.

What does seeking God wholeheartedly look like? Do I seek God with 50 percent of my heart? 75 percent? 25 percent? What would God say about my "seeking" percentage?

Does it matter? How?

King Hezekiah was a king. He needed to answer to no one. He needed to please no one but himself. He could use his time, resources, and talents to make his life better, more comfortable, or more exciting. He could have spent hour upon hour making sure that his every whim was satisfied, or spent time and treasure erecting monuments to himself so that future generations would remember his self-proclaimed greatness.

I could do the same. I could spend my time, my money, and my talents on what gives me the most in return.

I could concentrate on my "image" both for today and the future. I could try to make certain that I would not be forgotten. Then, one day, despite all my efforts, I could be forgotten.

Life is a vapor, a fog, a fading flower. Like the flower, I need to be one who is fragrant and attractive for the purposes of reproduction. Upon completion of my task, I will begin the fading, the drooping, the wilting that eventually lead to my death. Upon my death, this body that held me will slowly decay back to dirt, and eventually what I so cherished will be nothing more than a banquet for other life forms.

I will never be the one who ultimately measures my success. God will be the measurer; I will be the measured. He has told me what He will consider when evaluation time comes: my faith, demonstrated by my obedience.

What does this mean? This means that I *honestly believe*, not only in my words, but also in my life, that God is older than me, smarter than me, and loves me. That means that I adjust my thoughts and then my actions to agree with God, even if I lack understanding.

Sometimes, in this age of grace, I am careful not to force myself to live as I should. How stupid is that? When I face God, if I want to face Him with no regrets, I need to seek Him with all my heart, and work diligently at the plan He gives me, while constantly looking for Him to change the plan or give me another plan. In all I do, I need to roll up my sleeves, work hard, and trust Him. In this way alone will I succeed.

 Your life will demonstrate what you have faith in today. What will it say about what you believe? How do you know you are not lying to yourself?

Thought for Day 7

How should I live when my family disappoints me?

Genesis 37:3–7 (NLT)

3 Jacob loved Joseph more than any of his other children because Joseph had been born to him in his old age. So one day Jacob had a special gift made for Joseph—a beautiful robe.

4 But his brothers hated Joseph because their father loved him more than the rest of them. They couldn't say a kind word to him.

5 One night Joseph had a dream, and when he told his brothers about it, they hated him more than ever.

6 "Listen to this dream," he said.

7 "We were out in the field, tying up bundles of grain. Suddenly my bundle stood up, and your bundles all gathered around and bowed low before mine!"

What should Joseph expect from his family relationships?

Would it be right for his brothers to be happy for him because of their father's love for him? It would be right, but not necessarily human.

Can you imagine the battle that Joseph was placed into without even trying to be placed into a battle? Young

Joseph probably felt quite secure going to see his brothers. He probably felt wonderful about the coat of many colors given to him, and the chance he had to be a part of what his older brothers were doing. He was probably excited to see them and tell them about his life, what was going on at home, and about a dream he had.

The last thing he would probably be thinking was that his brothers would hate him just for *being*—for being a younger brother who was much loved by their father. In fact, I would bet that for Joseph, what his brothers were about to do to him was totally unthinkable. Yet it happened.

That was the day young Joseph began to grow up. That was the day he had to start dealing with the "depravity of man" issue. That was the day he began, no doubt, to spend long quiet times with God, trying to sort out what was happening. That was the day when his misery index created by false expectations began to increase.

So often, in my life, I expect too much from depraved humanity. So often, I think that those in my church—those Christians who seem to love God and family—are worthy of trust. They are not; only God is worthy of trust. When I trust humans too much, it is easy for me to lose trust in God. It is not God who fails; it is humans. It is not God who is depraved; it is humanity that is depraved.

When a person sins, when a leader falls, this should not be news. It should be news when a person makes the right choice, and when a leader does not sin. Depravity is not unusual; it is normal. Righteousness is unusual, unique, or holy. That is the goal: to be holy. Joseph had an opportunity at a young age to learn a lesson that all of us need to know and take to heart: God alone is faithful. God alone is worthy of our trust.

We want it to be different, but it is not. Do you trust in humans too much? Why? What will you have to do in your life to adjust your thinking?

_____

_____

_____

_____

_____

_____

_____

_____

_____

_____

_____

_____

_____

_____

_____

_____

Thought for Day 8

Why would God allow me to be kicked
when I am already down?

Genesis 39:2–4 (NLT)

2 THE LORD WAS WITH JOSEPH, SO HE SUCCEEDED IN
EVERYTHING HE DID AS HE SERVED IN THE HOME OF HIS
EGYPTIAN MASTER.

3 POTIPHAR NOTICED THIS AND REALIZED THAT THE
LORD WAS WITH JOSEPH, GIVING HIM SUCCESS IN EVERY-
THING HE DID.

4 THIS PLEASED POTIPHAR, SO HE SOON MADE JOSEPH
HIS PERSONAL ATTENDANT. HE PUT HIM IN CHARGE OF
HIS ENTIRE HOUSEHOLD AND EVERYTHING HE OWNED.

From total abandonment by those who were supposed
to be trustworthy, those he thought he could trust, to
absolute trust and authority in Potiphar's house. It
would only have been natural for Joseph to be thinking,
*Finally, now I will get somewhere; finally I have found
someone who believes in me, who trusts me, and who will
care for me.*

Then it happened again: the depravity thing kicked in.

Genesis 39:7–9 (NLT)

7 AND POTIPHAR'S WIFE SOON BEGAN TO LOOK AT HIM
LUSTFULLY. "COME AND SLEEP WITH ME," SHE DEMANDED.

8 But Joseph refused. "Look," he told her, "my master trusts me with everything in his entire household.

9 No one here has more authority than I do. He has held back nothing from me except you, because you are his wife. How could I do such a wicked thing? It would be a great sin against God."

Joseph, who by then had learned that he must control his actions and attitudes, because he had no control over anyone else's, was put in a very awkward and uncomfortable position. The good life he had begun to enjoy, for all the right reasons, was about to be taken away from him, for no apparently good reason. Joseph once again found himself betrayed by the very people whom he should have been able to trust. This event could have driven Joseph over the edge . . . or it could drive him to the only One who is worthy of trust.

Genesis 39:19–20 (NLT)

19 Potiphar was furious when he heard his wife's story about how Joseph had treated her.

20 So he took Joseph and threw him into the prison where the king's prisoners were held, and there he remained.

Joseph had been there before. He would be there again.

It is easy to expect people to be decent. It is easy to expect God to protect us if we are good, kind, hardworking, and loyal. It is easy to get discouraged when people deliver less than we expected (and they always do). It is during these times that we see what God can deliver. It is during the darkest times in life that God's light shines the brightest. I can either live in despair, waiting for humanity to change, or live in victory, in communion with an unchanging God. For now, the choice is mine.

Have you ever felt abandoned by God when in reality it was the depravity of humankind that was your problem? How will you or can you correct your thinking?

_____

_____

_____

_____

_____

_____

_____

_____

_____

_____

Thought for Day 9

What happens when I feel forgotten?

Genesis 40:13–14 (NLT)

13 Within three days Pharaoh will lift you up and restore you to your position as his chief cup-bearer.

14 And please remember me and do me a favor when things go well for you. Mention me to Pharaoh, so he might let me out of this place.

Finally a break! Some of Joseph's cellmates were going to have an audience before the king. Joseph was, once again, given some hope. I am sure he thought that these guys with whom he had shared a cell for so long would never forget their buddy when they stood before the king.

Genesis 40:20–23 (NLT)

20 Pharaoh's birthday came three days later, and he prepared a banquet for all his officials and staff. He summoned his chief cup-bearer and chief baker to join the other officials.

21 He then restored the chief cup-bearer to his former position, so he could again hand Pharaoh his cup.

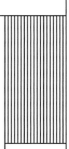

22 But Pharaoh impaled the chief baker, just as Joseph had predicted when he interpreted his dream.

23 Pharaoh's chief cup-bearer, however, forgot all about Joseph, never giving him another thought.

Once again, Joseph had his expectations crushed. Once again, a human had failed him.

How long can a man maintain a positive attitude when humanity keeps failing him? How long should Joseph hang on, and what does he have to hang onto? Nothing human, that is for sure.

I can only imagine the thoughts that went through Joseph's head as he waited moment after moment, hour after hour, day after day, for his buddy to tell the king of the injustice that was taking place in the prison. Of course, it did not happen.

Perhaps nothing is more devastating than being forgotten about. The cup-bearer, Joseph's buddy, forgot all about him, never even mentioning him. At least Joseph thought that his dad had probably never forgotten him. He probably knew that his brothers had never really forgotten him. He obviously thought that Potiphar's wife would not forget him.

To be forgotten has to be one of the most devastating thoughts of all: to believe that people are living their lives never thinking of you, acting as if you do not exist.

What was Joseph to do next? Well, perhaps Joseph could act like anyone would act who knows that God has not abandoned him. Perhaps Joseph could be the template for the true followers of God in the future. Perhaps Joseph could be the new Job, on display for all the heavenly host to notice and praise God for. I do not know what was going on in the innermost workings of Joseph's brain; I just know that God was moving him totally away from any trust, in any way, shape, or form, in humans or humanity. Joseph had a choice: to trust that God had a plan that was working through all of this, or to think that God had abandoned him. What he chose to believe made all the difference in the outcome.

What do you choose to believe about God when men and women all around you continually fail you? Are favorable circumstances the only criterion of God's observable love? What must you look at, if not the circumstances?

_____

_____

_____

_____

_____

_____

_____

_____

_____

Thought for Day 10

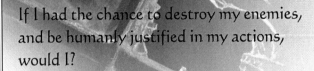

If I had the chance to destroy my enemies, and be humanly justified in my actions, would I?

Genesis 45:1–8 (NLT)

1 JOSEPH COULD STAND IT NO LONGER. THERE WERE MANY PEOPLE IN THE ROOM, AND HE SAID TO HIS ATTENDANTS, "OUT, ALL OF YOU!" SO HE WAS ALONE WITH HIS BROTHERS WHEN HE TOLD THEM WHO HE WAS.

2 THEN HE BROKE DOWN AND WEPT. HE WEPT SO LOUDLY THE EGYPTIANS COULD HEAR HIM, AND WORD OF IT QUICKLY CARRIED TO PHARAOH'S PALACE.

3 "I AM JOSEPH!" HE SAID TO HIS BROTHERS. "IS MY FATHER STILL ALIVE?" BUT HIS BROTHERS WERE SPEECH-LESS! THEY WERE STUNNED TO REALIZE THAT JOSEPH WAS STANDING THERE IN FRONT OF THEM.

4 "PLEASE, COME CLOSER," HE SAID TO THEM. SO THEY CAME CLOSER. AND HE SAID AGAIN, "I AM JOSEPH, YOUR BROTHER, WHOM YOU SOLD INTO SLAVERY IN EGYPT.

5 BUT DON'T BE UPSET, AND DON'T BE ANGRY WITH YOURSELVES FOR SELLING ME TO THIS PLACE. IT WAS GOD WHO SENT ME HERE AHEAD OF YOU TO PRESERVE YOUR LIVES.

6 THIS FAMINE THAT HAS RAVAGED THE LAND FOR TWO YEARS WILL LAST FIVE MORE YEARS, AND THERE WILL BE NEITHER PLOWING NOR HARVESTING.

7 GOD HAS SENT ME AHEAD OF YOU TO KEEP YOU AND YOUR FAMILIES ALIVE AND TO PRESERVE MANY SURVIVORS.

BEYOND THE EXPECTATIONS: Learning to Obey

8 So it was God who sent me here, not you! And he is the one who made me an adviser to Pharaoh — the manager of his entire palace and the governor of all Egypt.

What did Joseph learn during these years of turmoil? Perhaps he learned that humanity is depraved, and that God is the only one worthy of trust. Perhaps he learned that he could not control the attitudes and actions of others, but he could control his own attitudes and actions. Perhaps he learned that God has a plan that is much bigger than any person, so big that its very existence is often hardly distinguishable by humanity. Perhaps he learned that God's ultimate plan may involve misunderstandings, human disappointments, pain, suffering, and a huge misery index from unfulfilled expectations.

Joseph, in the end, did not take revenge on his sorry brothers, because he understood that God was bigger than all of them combined. Joseph was able, at least at this time, to have power and authority, because he knew that his power and authority were legitimate only if used for the good of others—even for the others who had tried to eliminate him.

Perhaps Joseph had had much time to think about his own depravity, and concluded that he was no less depraved than his brothers, Potiphar's wife, or the cup-bearer. Maybe that is why, when he eventually confronted them, he could do so with grace, mercy, and class.

Obviously, I do not know what-all went through Joseph's head, but I know that, in the end, he was a picture of mature spiritual leadership. His life could and should be studied for what one must know to age gracefully and lead with dignity. When all those around us are losing their heads, those who trust in God are not. When others are in despair because of broken dreams, hopes, and aspirations, those who trust in God are not. We do not write the final chapter; God does. It is our job to position ourselves to be in the final chapter, to be with Him in the victory circle, to speak as Joseph did, and to be able to proclaim honestly to those who hurt us, "What you meant for evil, God used for good."

Joseph knew that God was with him, even in his darkest moments, and he lived like anyone would live who knew God was with them.

Do you know that God is with you?
Do you live that way?

_____

_____

_____

_____

_____

_____

_____

_____

Thought for Day 11

Would I really trust God with what is most precious to me?

Genesis 22:1–2 (NLT)

1 SOME TIME LATER, GOD TESTED ABRAHAM'S FAITH. "ABRAHAM!" GOD CALLED. "YES," HE REPLIED. "HERE I AM."

2 "TAKE YOUR SON, YOUR ONLY SON—YES, ISAAC, WHOM YOU LOVE SO MUCH—AND GO TO THE LAND OF MORIAH. GO AND SACRIFICE HIM AS A BURNT OFFERING ON ONE OF THE MOUNTAINS, WHICH I WILL SHOW YOU."

I am sure this is not what Abraham expected to hear when he talked with God!

What am I expecting to hear from God today? Am I expecting God to tell me how I can live poverty free, anxiety free, or insult free? Am I expecting God to teach me how to make much out of my life, so I can be self-indulgent with what I have? What am I expecting to hear from Him?

In fact, do I even have my lines of communication open enough to hear what He is actually saying? Would God ever ask me to make a tremendous sacrifice? Would he ever ask me to place myself in a position that would compromise the safety of my family, friends, or nation? Would I even be open to His communication on these matters?

What if I owned a company, and God wanted to talk with me about plowing the profits—*all* of the profits—into helping the poor? What if God wanted to talk with me about letting go of my child, and encouraging him or her to serve God in a foreign and dangerous land? What if God wanted to speak to me about something I would consider absurd? Would I be willing to listen with an open heart?

I doubt it.

I have a long way to go in this respect. It seems, at times, as if there are certain subjects that are off limits for discussion. After all, these are the "sacred cows" that I have set up in my life; these are the things that prove God loves me; things that I have come to trust in as much as I trust in God.

Abraham was not being tested because God did not know how he was going to respond. I believe that Abraham was being tested so that *Abraham* would know what he truly believed. Humans can lie to themselves, so it is easy to say that we are dedicated to God, that we are desperate for Him, or that He is all we need—and then live as if none of that were true.

I have often heard people say that if they were million- aires, they would take care of the ministry in which I serve. I have thought that if I had tons of money, I surely would give it all away . . . but would I? I may never really know, and maybe I do not want to know. It is far easier to be poor and to say what I would do if I were rich, than to be rich and really know what I would do. Sometimes God needs to test us so that we can honestly evaluate ourselves, and I believe that this was what happened with Abraham and Isaac. Abraham was told that this miracle child was the child of promise. Abraham had a chance to show what he *really* believed about God's promise.

Abraham's reasonable expectations could have prevented him from listening to God. What "reasonable" expectations will prevent me or you from listening to God?

_____

_____

_____

_____

_____

_____

_____

_____

_____

_____

_____

_____

_____

_____

Thought for Day 12

What happens if God gives me a stupid assignment?

Ezekiel 2:1–7 (NLT)

1 "Stand up, son of man," said the voice. "I want to speak with you."

2 The Spirit came into me as he spoke, and he set me on my feet. I listened carefully to his words.

3 "Son of man," he said, "I am sending you to the nation of Israel, a rebellious nation that has rebelled against me. They and their ancestors have been rebelling against me to this very day.

4 They are a stubborn and hard-hearted people. But I am sending you to say to them, 'This is what the Sovereign Lord says!'

5 And whether they listen or refuse to listen— for remember, they are rebels—at least they will know they have had a prophet among them.

6 "Son of man, do not fear them or their words. Don't be afraid even though their threats surround you like nettles and briers and stinging scorpions. Do not be dismayed by their dark scowls, even though they are rebels.

7 You must give them my messages whether they listen or not. But they won't listen, for they are completely rebellious!"

What can I expect when God gives me an assignment? I would think that where God leads, God provides. I would think that if God is in it, great things will happen. I would think that if God sent me to a people to tell them about Him, those people would be prepared and ready to accept the message, and I would be received as a hero of sorts, a real genuine spiritual leader and mentor, a friend, or at least someone who is tolerable.

What happened here to Ezekiel?

God came to him, told him to go and speak to the people, and then went on to tell him that even though this was his assignment, and even though the words were directly from God, and even though what would be said would be good for the people, they would not listen to him.

I struggle with this, and I am not even Ezekiel. How could God give an assignment that He already knew would fail? (Here I go with my human thinking.) Why would God waste Ezekiel's life, talents, and resources by having him talk to people whom He knew would reject what Ezekiel said?

This was not for Ezekiel to answer. Ezekiel, like all humans, needed to listen to God. God knows what He is doing. God has a plan. God is God; Ezekiel was not. Ezekiel did exactly right by obeying God.

I am ashamed to say that sometimes I think about the apparent results more than about the obedience to God. The results of something are not for me to control; the obedience is. I need to put myself in a position to obey no matter what the results, for in that obedience I will find total freedom.

As God's servant, I must place myself in a position of subjection, not objection.

I often want to see results, even if I need to manufacture them, rather than remain obedient despite the results. How about you? Would you listen to God even if it seemed as though His orders were not producing results? Why or why not?

_____

_____

_____

_____

_____

_____

_____

_____

_____

_____

_____

_____

Thought for Day 13

Obedience is more important than understanding and the response of those to whom I minister.

Ezekiel 3:1–9 (NLT)

1 The voice said to me, "Son of man, eat what I am giving you—eat this scroll! Then go and give its message to the people of Israel."

2 So I opened my mouth, and he fed me the scroll.

3 "Fill your stomach with this," he said. And when I ate it, it tasted as sweet as honey in my mouth.

4 Then he said, "Son of man, go to the people of Israel and give them my messages.

5 I am not sending you to a foreign people whose language you cannot understand.

6 No, I am not sending you to people with strange and difficult speech. If I did, they would listen!

7 But the people of Israel won't listen to you any more than they listen to me! For the whole lot of them are hard-hearted and stubborn.

8 But look, I have made you as obstinate and hard-hearted as they are.

9 I have made your forehead as hard as the hardest rock! So don't be afraid of them or fear their angry looks, even though they are rebels."

Beyond the Expectations: Learning to Obey

Again, Ezekiel is given a message that could make any leader doubt and question. Ezekiel, in the end you will see two stubborn people running full speed into each other, and neither one will win, but both will get hurt. This does not seem to make sense.

Well, it does not make sense because I am thinking of things as I perceive them, instead of as they really are. In this passage, before God again tells Ezekiel about the lack of response he will encounter, He tells Ezekiel to take His Word, eat it, let it become one with him, let it symbolically sustain him, and let it be responsible for his very existence. So often, leaders are driven by their own goals, personal success, self-serving ideas, and public adulation. Ezekiel was to know God intimately, to allow God's Word to permeate his thinking, his actions, and all of his life. He was then to take the Word of God and deliver it, as it was, to the people, even while knowing that the people would not want to hear it and that, in fact, they would reject it.

God was faithful to Ezekiel. God was faithful to the people, even when he knew that the people would reject His message.

As a leader, I need to be totally in tune with God and His Word, not just with the responses of the people. I need to know who to listen to and who to be obedient to, no matter what the results. If God chooses me to be one who is able to change the world, so be it. If God wants to use me in a way so that no one ever hears my name, so be it. If I land somewhere in between, so be it. I must be dedicated to knowing God's Word and listening to it, regardless of what responses I receive. I must leave the results to God. I must not expect all who hear God's precious Word to respond favorably. Obedience is more important than understanding and response. I must never forget this.

Has God ever asked you to do something that seems irrational and unproductive? Are you willing to follow Him even if you do not understand Him?

_____

_____

_____

_____

_____

_____

_____

_____

_____

_____

_____

_____

_____

_____

_____

_____

Thought for Day 14

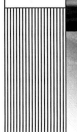

Is it possible to obey God and see no positive human results?

Ezekiel 3:16–17 (NLT)

16 AFTER SEVEN DAYS THE LORD GAVE ME A MESSAGE. HE SAID,

17 "SON OF MAN, I HAVE APPOINTED YOU AS A WATCHMAN FOR ISRAEL. WHENEVER YOU RECEIVE A MESSAGE FROM ME, WARN PEOPLE IMMEDIATELY."

I am sure Ezekiel must have struggled with his assignment. I know that I would be struggling and praying that God would allow me to see some fruit of my efforts. God, in EZEKIEL 3:16, gave Ezekiel another message, a message that may have helped clarify what was happening.

God told Ezekiel to be a watchman. Ezekiel knew what a watchman's job was, so this made some kind of sense to him. A watchman is, well, a watchman, the individual who stands and watches. When the watchman sees danger approaching, his job is to shout the warning to the ones who would do the defending. The watchman is not to put on his armor and go and try to defeat the enemy; he is to warn those who were trained in defeating the enemy.

God told Ezekiel that he was the watchman. He was to be the one who gave the warning, and he must take that

job seriously: if people actually listened to him, their lives could be saved. If they ignored him, there would be a tragic outcome.

However, Ezekiel, being a watchman, had much more to do than just watch. He understood the importance, once again, of actually watching: knowing what danger looked like so that he never became the watchman who cried "Wolf!" He needed to know what God would say, and know when to speak and when to remain silent. He needed to make sure that he did not sleep on his watch; if that happened, he could wake up and find that his negligence had caused total disaster.

Ezekiel's job was to watch. Ezekiel's job was to warn. Ezekiel's job was to hope. Ezekiel's job was to know God. Ezekiel's job was to listen to God. Ezekiel's job was to love the people by listening to God.

How easy it is to take on something that is not my job! How easy it is to fall asleep, when I should be watching. How easy it is to wallow in self-pity, and to leave my task undone, when I see no results.

I have not been called to live an easy life. I have been called to live an *obedient* life. This obedient life may cause me grief at times, but my grief is fueled by false expectations about the results of my obedience. It could be that my total surrender to God, my total obedience, brings me nothing but human sorrow and grief. Can I continue if that is all I see? Is obedience to God and knowing that I am pleasing Him enough?

 What is your job in life? Are you doing it? Are you even thinking about it? Will I be satisfied with the role God has given me?

BEYOND THE EXPECTATIONS: Learning to Obey

Thought for Day 15

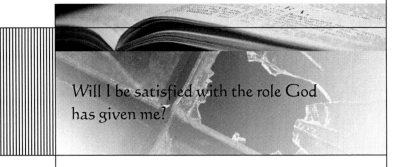

Will I be satisfied with the role God has given me?

Ezekiel 37:1–3 (NLT)

1 THE LORD TOOK HOLD OF ME, AND I WAS CARRIED AWAY BY THE SPIRIT OF THE LORD TO A VALLEY FILLED WITH BONES.

2 HE LED ME ALL AROUND AMONG THE BONES THAT COVERED THE VALLEY FLOOR. THEY WERE SCATTERED EVERYWHERE ACROSS THE GROUND AND WERE COMPLETELY DRIED OUT.

3 THEN HE ASKED ME, "SON OF MAN, CAN THESE BONES BECOME LIVING PEOPLE AGAIN?" "O SOVEREIGN LORD," I REPLIED, "YOU ALONE KNOW THE ANSWER TO THAT."

Ezekiel certainly had one of the more interesting lives in Scripture. I wonder what he was thinking as the Lord decided to grab him and go.

This time God spoke to him in a valley that was covered with bones. They were not small in number, nor were they new, for they were obviously old, dry, and lifeless.

Ezekiel might have looked over the valley and thought something like this: *Well, at least if he has me preach to dead bones, I will have the expected response. I know if I preach to these things, I can expect nothing, for they are nothing. There will finally be no disappointment in my assignment.*

I wonder why God chose this experience for Ezekiel. Could it be that Ezekiel saw what I have seen: that God kept giving him an impossible assignment so he just gave up, did what God said, but did not even hope for a good response? Did God bring Ezekiel here to show him that He could stir the souls of those he spoke to?

I do not know, and I do not know exactly what Ezekiel thought, but one line in these verses caught my attention: 3 "O Sovereign Lord," I replied, "you alone know the answer to that."

Ezekiel is at the point of total dependence on God; he simply accepted what God was going to do or not do. He realized that it was not up to him. He realized that his job was that of a watchman, not a reviver. He understood that his intimacy with God, his obedience to God, demonstrated his love and faithfulness to the people. He was not going to try to figure out what God was going to do; he was just going to go with Him, obey Him, and see what He did. And Ezekiel seemed fine with his role.

I too need to realize that I can focus on all of the disappointments in life, or I can focus on what God can do. Ezekiel knew that if God so desired, those bones could live and become a nation of people who loved and listened to Him. He knew that God is the ultimate power and authority in the universe. He had positioned himself to be a servant of the real King, and He was going to allow God to be God.

I need to be fine with the role God gives me. If I seem to be ministering to skeletons, I must know that He can make them live. If I am given an assignment, I must be faithful in that assignment. I cannot serve God because I expect God to fulfill my dreams. I need to serve God because He is God. He is older than me, smarter than me, and loves me. I can trust Him.

Are you fine with the role God has given you? What is holding you back?

_____

_____

_____

_____

_____

_____

_____

_____

_____

_____

_____

_____

_____

_____

_____

Thought for Day 16

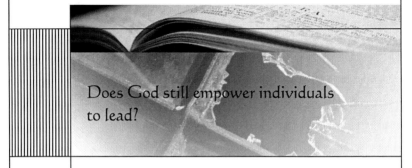

Does God still empower individuals
to lead?

Numbers 12:1–10 (NLT)

1 WHILE THEY WERE AT HAZEROTH, MIRIAM AND
AARON CRITICIZED MOSES BECAUSE HE HAD MARRIED A
CUSHITE WOMAN.

2 THEY SAID, "HAS THE LORD SPOKEN ONLY THROUGH
MOSES? HASN'T HE SPOKEN THROUGH US, TOO?" BUT THE
LORD HEARD THEM.

3 (NOW MOSES WAS VERY HUMBLE—MORE HUMBLE
THAN ANY OTHER PERSON ON EARTH.)

4 SO IMMEDIATELY THE LORD CALLED TO MOSES, AARON,
AND MIRIAM AND SAID, "GO OUT TO THE TABERNACLE,
ALL THREE OF YOU!" SO THE THREE OF THEM WENT TO
THE TABERNACLE.

5 THEN THE LORD DESCENDED IN THE PILLAR OF CLOUD
AND STOOD AT THE ENTRANCE OF THE TABERNACLE.
"AARON AND MIRIAM!" HE CALLED, AND THEY STEPPED
FORWARD.

6 AND THE LORD SAID TO THEM, "NOW LISTEN TO WHAT
I SAY: IF THERE WERE PROPHETS AMONG YOU, I, THE
LORD, WOULD REVEAL MYSELF IN VISIONS. I WOULD SPEAK
TO THEM IN DREAMS.

7 BUT NOT WITH MY SERVANT MOSES. OF ALL MY HOUSE,
HE IS THE ONE I TRUST.

8 I speak to him face to face, clearly, and not in riddles! He sees the Lord as he is. So why were you not afraid to criticize my servant Moses?"

9 The Lord was very angry with them, and he departed.

10 As the cloud moved from above the Tabernacle, there stood Miriam, her skin as white as snow from leprosy.

What were Aaron and Miriam expecting? As time went on, they obviously thought that Moses was not the only one who was favored or spoken to by God. They must have started to think of their own significance, their own positions, and their own importance to the mission.

This did not please God. God seems always to work through structure. He seems to honor those who honor those who are placed in leadership over them. Those who place themselves in a position of honor always lose.

Years ago, I remember my football coach talking to us as incoming freshmen. He told us that he never wanted to hear, from us, how good we were. He made it quite clear that if we were good at what we did, he would know about it, and he would know about it from someone other than us. He warned us against reading too much into the local papers that would one day make you out to be brilliant, and the next day be demanding your replacement. He reminded us that we were a part of a team, and that he, as our leader, would place people where they belonged, when they belonged there.

This sat well with some players. Other players would second-guess him, talk of favoritism, and generally begin small rebellions among the troops.

Miriam and Aaron were given a job to do in the nation of Israel. It was not the same job that Moses had. If they had truly been listening to God, they would have realized this and respectfully submitted to Moses. Instead, whomever they were listening to got them thinking of their own significance, and noticing that the people thought Moses was doing it all on his own, getting all the credit, and grabbing all the press. When they confronted Moses, things got ugly, both for Moses, who was just following God, and for them.

It really is not about status or position; it is about obedience. Who are you submitting to? How does that make you feel?

_____

_____

_____

_____

_____

_____

_____

_____

_____

_____

Thought for Day 17

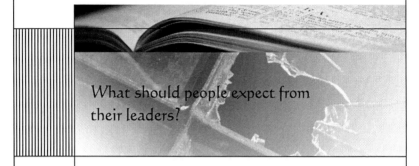

What should people expect from their leaders?

Deuteronomy 17:14–20 (NLT)

14 "You are about to enter the land the Lord your God is giving you. When you take it over and settle there, you may think, 'We should select a king to rule over us like the other nations around us.'

15 If this happens, be sure to select as king the man the Lord your God chooses. You must appoint a fellow Israelite; he may not be a foreigner.

16 "The king must not build up a large stable of horses for himself or send his people to Egypt to buy horses, for the Lord has told you, 'You must never return to Egypt.'

17 The king must not take many wives for himself, because they will turn his heart away from the Lord. And he must not accumulate large amounts of wealth in silver and gold for himself.

18 "When he sits on the throne as king, he must copy for himself this body of instruction on a scroll in the presence of the Levitical priests.

19 He must always keep that copy with him and read it daily as long as he lives. That way he will learn to fear the Lord his God by obeying all the terms of these instructions and decrees.

20 THIS REGULAR READING WILL PREVENT HIM FROM BECOMING PROUD AND ACTING AS IF HE IS ABOVE HIS FELLOW CITIZENS. IT WILL ALSO PREVENT HIM FROM TURNING AWAY FROM THESE COMMANDS IN THE SMALLEST WAY. AND IT WILL ENSURE THAT HE AND HIS DESCEN- DANTS WILL REIGN FOR MANY GENERATIONS IN ISRAEL.

What shall we expect from our leaders? What principles can I glean from this passage of Scripture?

I, as a leader, need to think about where my stability comes from. I am told in this passage where it does *not* come from. It does not come from my wealth, nor from my management of wealth. It does not come from my army, or from any accumulation of physical strength. It does not come from family, human relationships, or human alliances.

It comes from knowing and obeying God. Period.

If I am a leader that will be used by God, I am one who knows God's Word. The king, in this instance, was to write down, in his own writing, the law, in the very pres- ence of those who knew it, so that there would be no mistakes. Then, he was to make sure that he read it daily. Knowing it and reading it daily—it sounds so religious!

I do not know about you, but I told my wife that I loved her on our wedding day, and since nothing has changed, I do not need to tell her again. My children know that I love them, because I told them so twenty years ago. I do not really need to work on my relationship with Linda or my kids because, after all, the arrangement is permanent, and this type of permanent arrangement is good for my self-centeredness.

Those thoughts about my family are ridiculous, of course. If I am going to be a good husband, I am going to spend time with Linda. I am going to verbalize my commitment to her and my children, and I am going to do things daily that solidify my relationships, not estrange them. Likewise with God: If I am to be intimate with Him, that intimacy must include real time and real conversation. I have no other good alternative.

How important is your time with God? How well do you know the heart and mind of God?

_____

_____

_____

_____

_____

_____

_____

_____

_____

_____

_____

Thought for Day 18

What does one who is favored by God look like?

Luke 1:26–38 (NLT)

26 IN THE SIXTH MONTH OF ELIZABETH'S PREGNANCY, GOD SENT THE ANGEL GABRIEL TO NAZARETH, A VILLAGE IN GALILEE,

27 TO A VIRGIN NAMED MARY. SHE WAS ENGAGED TO BE MARRIED TO A MAN NAMED JOSEPH, A DESCENDANT OF KING DAVID.

28 GABRIEL APPEARED TO HER AND SAID, "GREETINGS, FAVORED WOMAN! THE LORD IS WITH YOU!"

29 CONFUSED AND DISTURBED, MARY TRIED TO THINK WHAT THE ANGEL COULD MEAN.

30 "DON'T BE AFRAID, MARY," THE ANGEL TOLD HER, "FOR YOU HAVE FOUND FAVOR WITH GOD!

31 YOU WILL CONCEIVE AND GIVE BIRTH TO A SON, AND YOU WILL NAME HIM JESUS.

32 HE WILL BE VERY GREAT AND WILL BE CALLED THE SON OF THE MOST HIGH. THE LORD GOD WILL GIVE HIM THE THRONE OF HIS ANCESTOR DAVID.

33 AND HE WILL REIGN OVER ISRAEL FOREVER; HIS KINGDOM WILL NEVER END!"

34 MARY ASKED THE ANGEL, "BUT HOW CAN THIS HAPPEN? I AM A VIRGIN."

35 The angel replied, "The Holy Spirit will come upon you, and the power of the Most High will overshadow you. So the baby to be born will be holy, and he will be called the Son of God.

36 What's more, your relative Elizabeth has become pregnant in her old age! People used to say she was barren, but she's now in her sixth month.

37 For nothing is impossible with God."

38 Mary responded, "I am the Lord's servant. May everything you have said about me come true." And then the angel left her.

What would I expect if God sent an angel to me today to inform me that I have been specially favored by God? Would I expect money, fortune, fame, health, or comfort?

Perhaps.

What did God's message mean for Mary? It meant that this young girl was to become pregnant outside the bounds of marriage. It meant talking with Joseph and convincing him and others that no sexual promiscuity had been involved. It meant that, for the rest of her life, she would see and hear the whispers of those around her accusing her of being one who "played around" and, as a result, gave birth to Jesus.

In fact, for Mary, in a human sense, the "blessing" of God seemed to be more of a curse than a blessing.

Unless, of course, we define *blessing* in the same way as God describes blessing. God's blessing may have nothing to do with wealth or comfort or popularity. In fact, we could be blessed of God and have nothing that this world offers. We could be blessed and be misunderstood, hated, despised, poor, sick, avoided, lonely, abandoned, and confused.

That hardly fits my human concept of blessing, but it is obviously true.

Are you blessed of God? How? How are you responding to His blessing?

_____

_____

_____

_____

_____

_____

_____

_____

_____

_____

_____

_____

_____

_____

Thought for Day 19

God's blessing may be wrapped in today's hardships.

Matthew 1:18–25 (NLT)

18 THIS IS HOW JESUS THE MESSIAH WAS BORN. HIS MOTHER, MARY, WAS ENGAGED TO BE MARRIED TO JOSEPH. BUT BEFORE THE MARRIAGE TOOK PLACE, WHILE SHE WAS STILL A VIRGIN, SHE BECAME PREGNANT THROUGH THE POWER OF THE HOLY SPIRIT.

19 JOSEPH, HER FIANCÉ, WAS A GOOD MAN AND DID NOT WANT TO DISGRACE HER PUBLICLY, SO HE DECIDED TO BREAK THE ENGAGEMENT QUIETLY.

20 AS HE CONSIDERED THIS, AN ANGEL OF THE LORD APPEARED TO HIM IN A DREAM. "JOSEPH, SON OF DAVID," THE ANGEL SAID, "DO NOT BE AFRAID TO TAKE MARY AS YOUR WIFE. FOR THE CHILD WITHIN HER WAS CONCEIVED BY THE HOLY SPIRIT.

21 AND SHE WILL HAVE A SON, AND YOU ARE TO NAME HIM JESUS, FOR HE WILL SAVE HIS PEOPLE FROM THEIR SINS."

22 ALL OF THIS OCCURRED TO FULFILL THE LORD'S MESSAGE THROUGH HIS PROPHET:

23 "LOOK! THE VIRGIN WILL CONCEIVE A CHILD! SHE WILL GIVE BIRTH TO A SON, AND THEY WILL CALL HIM IMMANUEL, WHICH MEANS 'GOD IS WITH US.'"

24 WHEN JOSEPH WOKE UP, HE DID AS THE ANGEL OF THE LORD COMMANDED AND TOOK MARY AS HIS WIFE.

25 BUT HE DID NOT HAVE SEXUAL RELATIONS WITH HER UNTIL HER SON WAS BORN. AND JOSEPH NAMED HIM JESUS.

Joseph had some real thinking to do. What can a man, who has been faithful to God, who had been sexually pure, expect from God? His reaction, when he found out about Mary's apparently "promiscuous" ways, was very human. I am sure there was tremendous disappointment, tremendous confusion, and tremendous doubts. These human disappointments were so great that God needed to intervene. Perhaps this was Joseph's "rooster crow," the moment when he knew, without any doubt, that God was indeed God, and was intimately involved in the affairs of humankind.

It was at this most difficult moment in history that Joseph understood. He knew not only that Mary had told him the truth, but also that he now needed to step up to the plate and be the leader God expected him to be. This may not have been his plan, or his expectation, but it was *the* plan—God's plan.

Joseph and Mary had to live with the looks and chatter of those who had no understanding of what was happening. They needed to travel to Joseph's home town to participate in a census, only to find out when they got there, that their own extended family was not going to extend the welcome mat. These two young people must have felt so alone, so misunderstood, and so needy.

That is, they might have felt that way until they started to put the pieces together; until they began to see that the very universe seemed to be responding to the birth of their son. Mary always knew, Joseph at some point was convinced, and both began to understand what God meant by "blessing."

Sometimes I remain confused as to what the blessing of God is all about. I ask God to bless, but then I think of Mary and Joseph, and I amend my request to meet my own limited understanding and expectation of blessing. Sometimes I just do not get it. To be blessed of God is to be used of God, not pampered by God. If God chooses to use me, what should I expect from Him?

_____

_____

_____

_____

_____

_____

_____

_____

_____

_____

_____

_____

Thought for Day 20

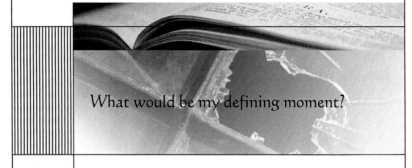

What would be my defining moment?

Luke 22:39–44 (NLT)

39 THEN, ACCOMPANIED BY THE DISCIPLES, JESUS
LEFT THE UPSTAIRS ROOM AND WENT AS USUAL TO THE
MOUNT OF OLIVES.

40 THERE HE TOLD THEM, "PRAY THAT YOU WILL NOT
GIVE IN TO TEMPTATION."

41 HE WALKED AWAY, ABOUT A STONE'S THROW, AND
KNELT DOWN AND PRAYED,

42 "FATHER, IF YOU ARE WILLING, PLEASE TAKE THIS
CUP OF SUFFERING AWAY FROM ME. YET I WANT YOUR
WILL TO BE DONE, NOT MINE."

43 THEN AN ANGEL FROM HEAVEN APPEARED AND
STRENGTHENED HIM.

44 HE PRAYED MORE FERVENTLY, AND HE WAS IN SUCH
AGONY OF SPIRIT THAT HIS SWEAT FELL TO THE GROUND
LIKE GREAT DROPS OF BLOOD.

What can I expect from God if I do everything right?
Can I expect comfort, ease, and popularity? No.

In this passage, Jesus struggles with His human desire to
take an easier route than the difficult, painful path God
is demanding. He prays, not for His will, but for God's

will to be accomplished. He asks if there is any other way to accomplish this, for He knows that He is going to be separated, for a moment in time, from His Father, and the thought of going through with it brings excruciating pain.

I was told that when a person sweats drops of blood, they are at the breaking point of human stress. Jesus wrestled with His obedience to the point where His human body actually began to break down.

When was the last time I struggled to that extreme point with wanting to follow God? Never.

Would I ever expect God to place me in a position where every fiber in my physical body and every brain cell in my human brain were screaming to do wrong? Would I expect, under such extreme conditions, to give in to disobedience and just claim that I could not physically or emotionally make the right decision?

Perhaps.

What factors went into Jesus Christ making the right decision here? Obviously, He was God, but He was also human. I too have God, in the form of the Holy Spirit, living in me. I too can wrestle with right and wrong. I too can give in to my human ways, or make myself totally available and obedient to God.

 I have never struggled to do right as intensely as Jesus struggled that night. Perhaps I have not made it to that time in life where God says, "This is your defining moment." Or perhaps I have already missed it. I wonder what it is?

Beyond the Expectations: Learning to Obey

Thought for Day 21

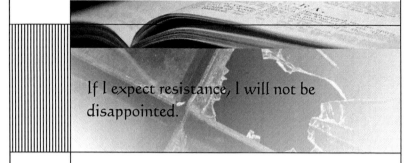

If I expect resistance, I will not be disappointed.

Mark 16:15 (NLT)

15 AND THEN HE TOLD THEM, "GO INTO ALL THE WORLD AND PREACH THE GOOD NEWS TO EVERYONE."

If I dedicate my life to going into the entire world and preaching the Good News, what can I expect?

I wonder what the disciples expected. They watched Jesus be misunderstood, falsely accused, hung on a cross, and in the end, be victorious. I wonder if they then felt that if they followed God, they would see the wonderful miracles they had seen while with Jesus, only this time they would see God use them to accomplish such things.

I wonder if they thought about the cost. I wonder if they thought about the rejection that was sure to be theirs. I wonder if they thought about the deaths they would face as they went to the world with the "Good News."

I think that at least some of them began to understand the real cost of discipleship. They saw that Jesus was willing to say no to all and every human instinct, in order to follow the King. They saw a plan unfold that was beyond human understanding. They saw that Jesus lived in the reality of another place and time in the universe. They saw the greatest enemy of man, death, conquered.

But did they know at this time what their commitment to Jesus was going to bring them? No.

Do I know, at this time, what intimacy with God and total obedience will bring me? No.

I *do* know that if I do everything as God directs, I can be hated, lied about, and physically and emotionally beat up. I do know that if I am in the center of God's will, I can expect Satan to unleash all he has against me. I do know that Satan will do all he can to stop me from intimacy with God and obedience to His will.

I can either accept the fact that this life I live will be a fight, or give in now and never really achieve the true blessing God has for me.

If I give in and live for now, I may have fewer bruises, but I will also have less satisfaction. I was not made to just live for now and enjoy this world. I was made to be a warrior, an intimate warrior. I am to make myself available to a King Who loves me, and, because of His grace, has decided to use me in the intense battles that take place on this side of eternity.

I can expect pain, sorrow, disappointment, and grief. I can also expect a victory one day, so splendid that all of the sorrow, disappointment, and grief will be but a distant memory. One day, as I play the role of intimate warrior, I will stand in victory with my King, and my obedience to Him will be the only thing that mattered. That day may be sooner than I think, so I must remain diligent.

 What will diligence look like in my life? Is the pain in my life due to obedience or disobedience?

BEYOND THE EXPECTATIONS: Learning to Obey

Final Thoughts

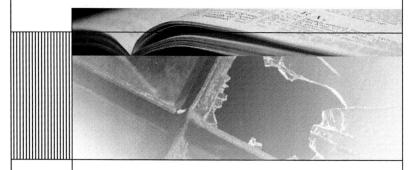

1 Peter 3:14 (NLT)

14 BUT EVEN IF YOU SUFFER FOR DOING WHAT IS RIGHT,
GOD WILL REWARD YOU FOR IT. SO DON'T WORRY OR BE
AFRAID OF THEIR THREATS.

The Bible makes it clear that those who are faithful
will gain reward. Those who listen to God, who live
their lives by faith, will be rewarded for their obedience.

So often, we seem to minimize or ignore the Bible's
teaching that God will reward the faithful. He will
not reward those whom I think are faithful. He will
reward those who are faithful as He has determined
what faithfulness is.

I think the reason we shy away from this is that we
do not like the idea that there will be some, who are
members of the family of God, who are not rewarded.
We do not want to think of the afterlife as a place
where some have more than others, or where some
are recognized more than others, and yet this is what
the Bible teaches.

God is clear, all through the Bible, that those who
obey will indeed be honored. I will admit that I do not
know what that means, but it does mean something.
I have heard teachers say that those who are faithful

will reign with Christ on earth during the millennium; others talk of crowns that we are given that allow us to honor God by giving them back; still others talk of both. Perhaps all of the above will happen.

Frankly, we could spend the rest of our lives in speculation about how God will reward the faithful. Or, we could just know that He will reward the faithful, and make sure that we are numbered among them.

I may not know all the specifics, but I can make my life's decisions based on what I do know. Therefore, I am going to choose to be an intimate warrior, an obedient servant, and a faithful friend. I need to concentrate today on doing well and being responsive to the Holy Spirit.

The end will take care of itself, for I will never be in a position to talk God into changing His mind about my service and attitude.

I can do something today, as long as I am alive, to make certain that I am rewarded one day by my King. I must choose today that path that leads to honoring my God, for tomorrow is guaranteed to no one.

God, help me to adjust my expectations to be in line with your expectations. Thank You for Your honest Word and its ability to pierce my heart and life. Help me today to honestly evaluate my life, actions, hopes, and dreams. You alone are God; I am your servant.

1 Corinthians 15:58 (NLT)

58 SO, MY DEAR BROTHERS AND SISTERS, BE STRONG AND IMMOVABLE. ALWAYS WORK ENTHUSIASTICALLY FOR THE LORD, FOR YOU KNOW THAT NOTHING YOU DO FOR THE LORD IS EVER USELESS.

Silver Birch Ranch
"To Know Christ and To Make Him Known"

Silver Birch Ranch has been serving our nation's youth since the summer of 1968. Its unique location allows children and families to enjoy swimming, horseback riding, white water rafting and more, while being challenged to understand and respond to God's plan for their lives.

Silver Birch Ranch also hosts year-round conferences and retreats for churches, and a Bible college, the Nicolet Bible Institute.

Silver Birch Ranch has many materials to help you in your effort to be intimate with God and family. Through the Omega Force program, you can receive materials that will help you with your personal walk with God, and remind you to live your life with "no regrets."

For information about Silver Birch Ranch, Nicolet Bible Institute, and the Omega Force program, please visit our web site at www.silverbirchranch.org.

If you are interested in inviting Dave Wager as a speaker for your special event, please contact him at Silver Birch Ranch, N6120 Sawyer Lake Road, White Lake, WI 54491, or by email at dave.wager@silverbirchranch.org.

Additional Books, Resources, and Services Available from Grace Acres Press

Other Intimate Warrior Titles by Dave Wager
Beyond the Resistance: Learning to Face Adversity
Beyond the Resistance Study Guide
Beyond the Compass: Learning to See the Unseen
Beyond the Compass Study Guide
Beyond the Deception: Learning to Defend the Truth
Beyond the Deception Study Guide

Other Titles from Grace Acres Press
Life Before Death: A Restored, Regenerated, and Renewed Life by Ian Leitch; Foreword by Joseph M. Stowell, Moody Bible Institute (retired)

Growing Up Yanomamö: Missionary Adventures in the Amazon Rainforest by Mike Dawson; Foreword by Larry M. Brown, New Tribes Mission

Strengthened by Grace: A Systematic Theology Handbook by Richard E. Wager; Foreword by Art Rorheim, Awana International

Honest Questions Deserve Honest Answers: Lessons in Apologetics DVD by Ian Leitch

Also Available from Grace Acres Press
- Author presentations
- Book excerpts for your newsletters
- Fundraising programs
- Writing seminars—elementary school through adults
- Publishing seminars and consulting

Call today 888-700-GRACE (4722)
or visit our Web site:
www.GraceAcresPress.com
P.O. Box 22
Larkspur, CO 80118